Garden
Paths & Stepping Stones

Garden Paths

& Stepping Stones

Tara Dillard

Sterling Publishing Co., Inc.

New York

Prolific Impressions Production Staff:

Editor in Chief: **Mickey Baskett**

Creative Director: **Joel Tressler**

Graphics/Photography: **Joel Tressler**

Administration: **Jim Baskett**

Library of Congress Cataloging-in-Publication Data

Dillard, Tara.
    Garden paths & stepping stones / Tara Dillard.
        p. cm.
    Includes index.
    ISBN-13: 978-1-4027-1469-6
    ISBN-10: 1-4027-1469-6
1. Garden walks. 2. Landscape gardening. I. Title. II. Title: Garden paths and stepping stones.

TH4970.D55 2006
712'.6--dc22

                                                                2006032787

2 4 6 8 10 9 7 5 3 1

Published by Sterling Publishing Co., Inc.
387 Park Avenue south, New York, N.Y. 10016

©2007 Prolific Impressions, Inc.

Produced by Prolific Impressions, Inc.
160 South Candler St., Decatur, GA 30030

Distributed in Canada by Sterling Publishing
c/o Manda Group, 165 Dufferin Street
Toronto, Ontario, Canada M6K 3H6
Distributed in the United Kingdom by GMC Distribution Services,
Castle Place, 166 High Street, Lewes, East Sussex, England BN7 1XU
Distributed in Australia by Capricorn Link (Australia) Pty. Ltd.
P.O. Box 704, Windsor, NSW 2756 Australia

Printed in China
All rights reserved
Sterling   ISBN-13: 978-1-4027-1469-6
           ISBN-10: 1-4027-1469-6

For information about custom editions, special sales, premium and corporate purchases, please contact Sterling Special Sales Department at 800-805-5489 or specialsales@sterlingpub.com.

IN MEMORY OF DAVID STEVENS

About the Author

Tara Dillard gardens in the Southern United States, a climate suited to gardening all year. She hosted a garden show on CBS and appeared many times on NBC, HGTV and PBS. With degrees in Engineering and Horticulture, she has won national awards for writing, speaking and designing. Additionally, she is a regular instructor at Atlanta Botanical Garden, Gwinnett College, and Georgia Master Gardeners. Tara lectures nationally and passionately believes that beautiful gardens improve lives.

Other books by TARA DILLARD...

THE GARDEN VIEW: Designs for Beautiful Landscapes
BEAUTIFUL BY DESIGN: Stunning Blueprints for Harmonious Gardens

With Gratitude...

Dana McPhearson & Bill Brown, Terri Rooks & Jo Anne Hall, Phyllis & Tom Reetz, Kelley Dillard, Joel & Ellen Tressler, Robert Norris, Shannon Pable, Lysa Jacobus, Ellen Ungashick, Carolyn Baker, Michelle Stewart, Bill Hudgins & Lush Life, Ellie Smith, Audrey Newsome, Rhonda Latif, Renee & Denny Hopf, Sam & Carleen Jones of Piccadilly Farm, Dana & Tom Curtis, Kay & Don Connelly, Danielle & Keenan R.S. Nix, Marion Munagian, Alicia & Andy LaRocco, Marifae & Frank Jones, Nora Munagian & Mark Norton, Susie & Dave Deiters, Kent Richards, Ron Schneiberg and Unlimited Landscaping, David Stevens, Mary Kistner Center, Peggy Moss and Vines Botanical Garden, Eric Shaw, The Carl House in Auburn Georgia, Geri Laufer and the Atlanta Botanical Garden, Ricky Ballin and AYS Lawn Care and Landscaping, Dan & Mike Perry and Atlanta Lanscape Materials, Judy Mozen & Randy Urquhart, Anna & Vernon Davis.

TABLE OF CONTENTS

It's interesting looking at the recent fifty years of garden books to learn about garden paths. The indexes typically list "paths," books prior to that time index "walks" not "paths." The archaic form of the word walk means "to be in motion" and is further defined as moving on foot for pleasure or exercise. Large estate gardens, that are over a century old, have pleasure walks. They meander like rivers past interesting plants, focal points and beautiful views. Pleasure walks were a form of entertainment, exercise and socializing during eras without TV, radio, computer, Internet, headphones or telephones.

Paths are succinctly described as a track frequently used by man or beast. In our multi-tasking age, we only have time for frequently used paths - functional paths from driveway to backdoor or street to front door. The most important paths, to front and back doors, are usually built with the house. Other paths we get to build. Paths begin with function - going to the garbage can, woodpile, vegetable garden, dog run, places you visit frequently. Choices of path making are joyful. You decide where new paths will go and what they will be made of. Transforming necessity into art.

A house with garden paths creates its own geography. Garden paths you build will do more than just get you to your destination they will combine art, fate and character.

"You can't be so sophisticated or you just dry up."

– Lee Bontecou

PICTURED RIGHT: A curved walking path intensifies the "eye-sweet" line by being lower than the plantings surrounding it and contrasting in color.

Pathway History

"It is a matter of putting your brain, your eye and your heart in the same line of sight."

– Henri Cartier-Bresson

In the Beginning

In the beginning paths were made by animals. They are still making paths. Their paths are functional and beautiful. Traveling from a sleeping place to food sources, animals wear paths through woods or grassy plains, veering around rocks, steep slopes, roots or holes creating paths with broad curves. Landscape architects call this curve the "eye-sweet" line. Many paved roads were originally animal paths. The "eye-sweet" line has evolved as the best for curving garden paths on several continents, in many cultures and through thousands of years of garden path making. The few exceptions, extremely wavy garden paths, did not last long in any known histories. Multi-culturally, ancient Man discovered extremely wavy garden paths were not easy to maintain nor sufficiently beautiful to earn the effort of maintenance.

ABOVE: Deer carved this woodland path from repeated and continuous use.

OPPOSITE: A meandering path through a woodland leading to a sunny meadow; this path was created by cows. The curve of animal paths is called the "eye-sweet" line by landscape architects. A desirable line for your own garden paths.

ABOVE: Intensification of the "eye-sweet" line. Progressing from formal ornamental plantings, at the curve of plantings in the right of the picture, to a lower mown curve of meadow in the middle for easy walking, transitioning to taller meadow at the left.

RIGHT: A formal "eye-sweet" line. A curving path deer or cows might create but dressed up with bricks and ornamental plantings.

In the Beginning

Clues remain, dating to 8000 BC, about cultivated land in Jericho. Farming can be traced to 6500 BC near Iran/Iraq. Egypt and China have records of farming dating to 5000 BC. Cuneiform tablets, dated 4000 BC, describe a garden in Mesopotamia, precious water was delivered via canals, aqueducts and rills, influencing the layout of geometric gardens with straight paths. India and South America extensively cultivated their lands by at least 2500 BC. There were hanging gardens in Babylon, capital of Sumeria, by 2250 BC; they were pleasure gardens, naturalistic in design, indicating an improved economic environment. Spirituality was an element of Babylonian hanging gardens; pathways meandered and were meant to be contemplative, ennobling and revelatory.

Greek gardening, well established with the leisure class, was written about in Homer's Odyssey, 800 BC. The Romans absorbed lessons from Greek gardeners and brought those ideas to delectable levels by 200 BC. They were also the first to recognize the need to combine their homes with a garden. From 200 BC to the height of the European Renaissance, 1400-1600, Roman garden ideas were the golden template to follow.

ABOVE: Not formal and not completely natural. This curving path, through woods, has been dressed up with woodland plants and the trees have had their lower branches pruned for aesthetics and filtered light.

When Mughal emperor Mohammed Babar (1483-1530) brought the Central Asian method of irrigation to India he also brought the Persian word *bagh*, meaning house-and-garden. His own home he named Ram Bagh. A home is tied to its garden with paths.

Only four mughals later, Shah Johan (1628-1658) built a memorial garden for his empress, Mumtaz-Mahal. Straight garden paths dominate the garden breaking it into quadrants, each quadrant with beautiful geometric patterns within. We know the garden today as the Taj Mahal.

"...wide places for walking with all kinds of sweet fruit trees, laden with fruit, a sacred way, beautiful with flowers of all lands."

- Tablet recording a garden of Ramses III, 1198-1166 BC

The pattern of ancient gardening from subsistence farming to artistic pleasure gardening has been repeated many times during the known 10,000 years of garden history. Garden pathways follow that pattern, straight paths for subsistence farming to a mix of straight and curving paths for pleasure gardening.

ABOVE LEFT: Transitioning informality, from lawn to evergreen groundcovers at the start of the path, to moss, to woodland. Most paths traveling from formal to informal will have at least three regions: formal, informal, and very informal.

LEFT: A simple path, not done simply. Laying stones in concrete makes a path appear more formal; square or rectangular cut stones are more formal than irregularly shaped stones. Humor emanates from this path with its whimsical style of laying the edges.

OPPOSITE PAGE: Evocative of nature with obvious embellishments; a simple wood bridge, limbing-up of trees and nurturing of the fern glade. Imagine this same woodland with the path made of flagstones, edged with brick, and the bridge having handrails. Simple changes create big effects in the aesthetics of the garden.

"...well-laid garden plots have been arranged, blooming all the year with flowers."

– Homer, 800 B.C.

"The work of art comes into being through the artistic evaluation of its elements...only forming is essential."

– Kurt Schwitters

10,000 Years of Garden Paths

🌿 Animals make paths with broad sweeping curves that landscape architects call the "eye-sweet" line--a very desirable pathway curve.

🌿 Extremely wavy garden paths are undesirable and have not survived long in any known histories.

🌿 8000 BC - signs of cultivated land in Jericho.

🌿 6500 BC - signs of farming in Iran/Iraq.

🌿 5000 BC - signs of farming in Egypt and China.

ABOVE AND PAGE 20: Two views of the same table, seen from different paths each path with its own drama, character and elegance. Garden paths are a great design tool allowing you to make one focal point, a focal point from several directions. This garden and its paths have reached the level of art.

🌿 4000 BC - cuneiform tablets from Mesopotamia describe a garden with irrigation, canals, and straight garden paths.

🌿 2500 BC - extensive cultivation of land in India and South America.

🌿 2250 BC - hanging gardens in Babylon are naturalistic with curving garden paths.

🌿 800 BC - Homer wrote about a garden in the Odyssey.

🌿 200 BC to 1600 AD - Roman garden ideas widely absorbed.

🌿 Mohammed Babar (1483-1530) brought the Persian word *bagh*, meaning house-and-garden, to India. This spread the idea that houses and gardens are tied together with paths.

🌿 Shah Johan (1628-1658) builds Taj Mahal. The style is of straight garden paths enclosing quadrants with intricate geometry.

"Consult the genius of the place in all."

- Alexander Pope

ABOVE: A formal path, less formal during summer with
lush foliage and formal again with the bones of winter
having overtaken the lushness.

🌿 Eastern garden ideas began movement to the West in the early 18th century with
expanded shipping and the success of missionaries embedded in the East.
China and Japan were creating curving garden paths centuries before the West.

🌿 Englishmen, "Capability" Brown (1715-1783) and Humphrey Repton (1752-
1818) destroyed ancient gardens with straight paths to create naturalistic gardens
with curving paths.

🌿 Englishwoman, Gertrude Jekyll (1843-1932) created gardens having both formal
areas with straight garden paths and woodland gardens having garden paths with
natural broad curves. A dying Empire spread her garden ideas over most of the
globe.

🌿 1930'S- present - Hollywood has spread garden ideas. 1950's- present - multi-
media spread of garden ideas. Today, instant digital images, the Internet and its
search engines are yet a new way the world is learning about garden styles.

Designing a Pathway

"A garden that is not beautiful in winter is not a beautiful garden."

– Jacques Wirtz

Put it on Paper

Pathways are important to a garden and how they are tied to your house. They should be the first element of design when planning your garden. Draw a birds-eye view sketch, not to scale is fine, of your garden and home. Include the house, patio/deck, existing sidewalks, driveway, trees and large shrubs that will remain. Make 75 copies so you will have plenty of pages to play with as you sketch your ideas.

Tear out dozens of magazine pictures of garden paths you like. You'll notice that there is a common thread with the pictures; you have found your favorite garden path style. Be bold. Copy your favorite garden path style and have fun recapitulating within your constraints.

ABOVE & OPPOSITE: A mother and a grandmother luring their young along the path to a love of gardening. Color and whimsy rule. Round cement stepping stones have been given a mosaic treatment.

Designing a Pathway

TOP LEFT: Classic, formal roundabout. Imagine this same garden with a fountain at the center and benches placed at the edge of the path facing the fountain. Examining how many ways it can be modified, without changing its structure, tests for good garden style. The existing path invites you to enjoy but keep moving. Adding benches, inviting you to stop and enjoy the area creates a big change, but simply.

ABOVE: Pathways and roundabouts go together. Whenever you have two pathways intersecting add extra space at the intersection, creating your own roundabout. Roundabouts create a place at their center for a focal point. It is no accident where these two paths intersect, on axis with the door.

LEFT: A pathway ending at a small patio yet not so small that it feels like a dead-end. Avoid dead-ends, if possible, with your pathways.

ABOVE & RIGHT: The same stepping stone path from opposite directions. This path is a magician, hiding focal points from one direction while showing them off in another. Make magicians of your paths.

Pathways should be functional, leading to necessities or follies, not dead-ends. When designing your garden begin by placing paths. Don't consider anything else during this phase except your favorite garden path pictures. Have fun, you've got 75 copies to play with sketching paths. If you like more than one of your sketches it's time to layout string on your property to see your ideas in three-dimension. Some of your good ideas will kill themselves immediately when laid out in three-dimension, don't worry, that's common going from one-dimension on paper to three-dimension in your garden.

If you like how the string looks on your property, keep it there for a couple of weeks so you can "live" with your new paths before they're built. It is much easier to move string than bricks, stones or concrete. For a curving path, hose, rope, or spray paint can mark the layout of a path. Home improvement stores sell kits with string and pins that are best to use if laying out a straighter path.

Traffic Flow

Foot traffic should flow around your entire property. Children know this; they play around their entire house even if they have to climb a fence to do so. As adults we are reminded of what we knew as children when we are in beautiful gardens with flowing paths.

The pathway you design should be no less than two feet wide – a one-person width. A four foot wide path is the minimum width for allowing two people to walk side by side. A utilitarian walkway which you will use for moving garden equipment should be at least three feet wide.

The width of your path will determine how quickly the feet can travel, and your intention for the path. A wide, straight walk will allow the pedestrian to travel more quickly. A narrower path will cause the walker to move more slowly and look down more often.

ABOVE: An aesthetic path and a functional path used by the gardener while maintaining the perennial border. Stones set in turf are easier to maintain if the turf is a clumping grass like fescue. Stones set in running grasses like centipede will need the weed-eater.

ABOVE: Formality on the way to a greenhouse. A stone retaining wall and pea gravel path complementing each other. The richness of the curved steps, protruding into the path, announce, "yes, you're allowed, please come see my greenhouse." There are many ways a pathway speaks without uttering a word.

ABOVE: Wherever you need to go in your garden, build yourself a path. This gardener needs to walk to a potting shed created under a deck.

LEFT: This house and garden came with a brick patio and concrete driveway but no path connecting the two. Choosing stone for combining the areas was wise; it doesn't compete with either the brick or concrete, instead it's a good companion.

ABOVE LEFT: Without this stepping stone path there would be no way for the homeowner to get from her back yard to front yard on this side of her home.

ABOVE RIGHT: Tiny area with a major confluence of path and water drainage. Here, a stone path leads to a wood bridge and to a pine straw path. The bridge crosses a dry streambed. It was never a real stream but manmade to channel rainwater. Rainwater travels where it needs to go and so does foot traffic.

Atlanta Botanical Garden

"Imagination is more important than knowledge."

– Albert Einstein

Choosing Path Material

Consider safety when choosing pathway materials. You may find a free cache of jagged or slick stones but they should not be considered for walking on, as path edging they are perfect. Heavy traffic patterns in your garden should have strong and durable materials, brick or stone, while a path to your compost pile may be a bit of mulch or a ribbon of compacted dirt.

Choose path materials that require little upkeep; low maintenance gardening includes wise choices for pathways, plants, focal points and furniture.

Paths should have the personality of your house. Choose materials that are compatible with the style of your house. Informal cottage or farmhouse styles could use materials such as pea gravel or crushed stone. Formal style houses would be harmonious with paths of brick or cut stone for example.

ABOVE: Formal brick path in a public garden. If the soldiers were raised people might trip. Public gardens are more likely to have two to three people walking abreast than private gardens.

"The 7th fine art-gardening, not horticulture,
but the art of embellishing ground by fancy."

– Thomas Jefferson

Choosing materials for a path can carry a lot of emotional baggage. You might like the crunching sound of a pea gravel path but have land too steep. Stone is making your heart pulsate with desire but your region doesn't have stone, making it a very expensive option. A lawn pathway is your aesthetic ideal but parts of it are compacted and dead because of heavy use by you, children, dogs or shade. A pathway running in a direction feet won't follow isn't really a pathway.

Take your time designing pathways. Be practical in planning and implementing your pathways, not emotional. It might be helpful to hire a garden designer, for one hour, to review your plans or have a gardening friend look them over.

ABOVE: This path creates its own garden room. Most things you do in a garden require patience to achieve. This path, with massive stonework and generous gravel, if copied, will create the same look the same day you lay the stone and gravel. You'll only have to wait for your plantings to grow.

29

"What I am actually saying is that we need to be willing to let our intuition guide us, and then be willing to follow that guidance directly and fearlessly."

– Shakti Gawain

Atlanta Botanical Garden

Garden Path Materials Considerations

1. Living paths: lawns, meadows, groundcovers.

2. Organic mulch paths: pine straw, shredded leaves, shredded bark, cocoa shells.

3. Inorganic mulch paths: shredded tires, old shingles, old carpeting.

4. Vegetable garden paths: newspaper, carpeting, card board, gravel, wood chips.

5. Gravel paths: rounded pea gravel, small, medium, large; jagged stone gravel, small, medium, large.

6. Stone: many types.

7. Brick: matching house, without holes.

8. Wood: railroad ties, pressure treated, tree limbs.

9. Concrete: stamped, stained, poured, ready-made squares and interlocking pavers.

10. Mix path materials: brick edged with stone, mulch edged with brick, gravel edged with brick and etc.

TOP: A path made of crushed brick.

ABOVE: More than just a dirt path, colored glass has been dug in to help light the way for fairies.

"Make no little plans;
they have no magic to stir
men's blood...Make big
plans, aim high in hope,
and work."

– Daniel H. Burnham

Mixing Path Materials and Styles

Form, function and availability have converged in garden path making for thousands of years. Necessity forced Eastern gardeners in 300BC to create paths of stone, gravel and sand. Not able to afford an entirely stone path, gravel was added creating a style copied today. Gravel paths edged with stone or brick are classic. Stone paths edged with brick are classic. Mulch paths edged with stone or tree limbs have a long history.

ABOVE: Pathway view from a front door. Mixing several materials yet remaining cohesive.

RIGHT: A mix of stone and gravel. Diagonal stones make a narrow path appear wider.

Designing a Pathway

Pathways in a garden are best if the diversity of materials is kept minimal. Yes, contrasting texture is important in garden design but so is repetition. Garden paths tie a garden together, and your house to the garden, repetition of path materials is important. Make this tough rule more generous by pushing its limits. Push the limits of any garden design rule. A solid brick path can lead to a flagstone path edged with brick, leading to a gravel path edged with flagstone ending at a wood chip path edged with brick. Create repetition within a diversity of materials.

ABOVE: Fine gravel, edged with cobblestone soldiers, leading to a front door.

OPPOSITE: Pathways and lawns make great canvasses for creating seasonal shadows. Watching shadows play across your paths throughout the year is a subtle enjoyment.

Designing a Pathway

We have over 10,000 years of garden path ideas to choose from. It is common to see influences from several different eras and cultures in most gardens, even small gardens. Jekyll's idea of multiple garden rooms is popular because it allows you to have a Japanese garden room, a rococo garden room, a folk art garden room, a Persian garden room or more. Flowing ingeniously together, with paths integrating the entire garden.

Looking at garden path styles through the centuries quickly exposes what materials the paths were made of. Garden paths are made of what is readily available, inexpensive and not labor intensive. Those facts haven't changed in thousands of years.

ABOVE: A woodland style garden with very formal underpinnings. The understory tree at the right front of the path has been pruned to expose its branching pattern more artistically. Plantings have been carefully chosen to shock with their contrasting shapes and colors. A focal point has been placed seductively at the end of a long curve. The insouciant formality of the pink foxglove makes me imagine it was planted by the wind, the ultimate in natural gardening. The path caresses the feet and ankles with low, lush plantings.

ABOVE: Formal and informal, straight yet curving at the far end. This path has it all, making you want to turn left, midway, onto the stepping stone path and wanting to go straight to see what's beyond the curve. The combination of gravel path with cobblestone edging and plants oozing beyond their border into the path add the air of informality. The formality of the straight path with stone edging allows for semi-negligent maintenance. A great secret of many formal garden paths, they allow you to be slightly sloppy with maintenance because the eye picks up the clean lines of the path.

"The adventure the hero is ready for is the adventure he gets."

– Joseph Campbell

ABOVE: This brick patio was enlarged using stone, which mixes well with brick. The stones taper slightly toward the outdoor fireplace. What began as a simple back yard has become an outdoor dining room.

Pathway Design Considerations:

🌿 Pathways should be the first element designed into your garden.

🌿 Draw a birds-eye view sketch of your house, driveway, existing paths, patio/deck and property lines.

🌿 Tear out dozens of garden path pictures you like from magazines.

🌿 Be bold; recapitulate your favorite garden paths into your garden sketch.

🌿 Foot traffic should flow around your entire property.

"There are many ways a pathway speaks without uttering a word."

Pathways in Garden Design

🌿 Pathways should be functional, leading to necessities or follies, not dead-ends.

🌿 Use string to lay out your path ideas.

🌿 Live with a string liner path a couple of weeks before building your path.

🌿 String is much easier to move than stone, bricks or concrete.

ABOVE: This is not a good stone path for heavy foot traffic but perfect for light use, and viewing from the house. Irregularly shaped stones, with jagged edges, may cause tripping. Along with simplicity choose safety.

ABOVE: A new path being created through the woods with its direction already determined by deer.

Pathway Design Considerations:

🌿 House and garden should be related or harmonious in materials.

🌿 Garden paths tie a house to its garden.

🌿 Garden paths tie a garden together.

🌿 Contrasting texture is important in garden design.

🌿 Repetition is important in garden design.

Pathway Design Considerations:

- Diversity of pathway materials should be kept minimal.

- Create repetition within a diversity of materials.

- Push the limits of any garden design rule.

- Brick paths can lead to stone paths edged with brick, leading to a gravel path edged with stone, leading to a mulch path edged with stone.

- Gray flagstone is classic. It is durable and looks good with a simple log cabin or a formal Georgian manor.

- If brick or stone is too expensive, use it for edging a cheaper gravel path.

- Consider safety – jagged or slick stones should be used for edging not walking.

- Busy paths should be made of durable materials like brick or stone.

- Infrequently used paths can be simple, use mulch.

- Choose path materials that require little upkeep.

Pathway Soldiers

"Never allow the foot to take the path already taken by the eye."

– Rosemary Verey

When a path has edging, the edging pieces are called soldiers. A wood chip path edged with tree limbs, and a flagstone path edged with cobblestones both have soldiers – just different types. Soldiers give a finished look to a pathway and make a pathway have more emphasis. For some paths, soldiers are functional, helping to keep wood chips or gravel from spreading.

How high a soldier rises above its path influences how formal a path will appear. A brick soldier, flush with its path, is informal relative to the same brick soldier raised two inches higher. It is not uncommon for a garden to have several types of soldiers just as it has several types of paths.

RIGHT: Stone soldiers dress up this pea gravel path and also help keep it within bounds.

OPPOSITE: Soldiers along this path are so large and raised so high, the path appears to be a bridge.

ABOVE: Soldiers that are raised make a path appear more formal.

Pathway Soldier Tools:

- Long handled garden shovel with round nose
- Garden shovel with square nose
- Pick or adz to loosen packed dirt
- Level

Installing Soldiers

1. Clear the area for your path and dig a level path about three inches deep in the earth.

2. Dig a trench along the sides of your path to the depth and width needed to accomodate the type of soldiers you are using. Use a level to make sure trench is even.

3. Place soldiers in the trench.

4. Pack loose soil around the soldiers and tamp (see photo 1.)

5. Finish soldiers by gently watering.

ABOVE: Placing soldiers and the finished path.

"To live a creative life, we must lose our fear of being wrong."

— Norman Mailer

ABOVE: Here stone soldiers and pinestraw mulch contrast with the shredded mulch of the path itself. This path wouldn't be as showy without its soldiers. You may dislike this path now but in three years when the plantings are cascading over the soldiers, you might want to copy it.

Living Paths

Lawns are Living Paths

Expanses of turf allow for foot traffic in myriad choices of direction. Lawn selections vary by region; and within an individual region there are usually several choices. Choose the correct lawn according to the amount of sun/shade you have and the amount of foot traffic it will receive.

Children's play areas need spreading grasses in a sunny area, clumping grasses don't rejuvenate easily after abuse. If the play area is in shade a soft mulch is best because of limited choices for shady lawns that handle high foot volume.

If you are able to decide what type of lawn you want, versus inheriting a lawn with your home, consider many factors. Some lawns are evergreen, others go dormant for a season. Some lawns clump while others spread. Various types of grasses have specific soil and light requirements. Choose the type of grass that suits your needs and environment. Once decided, you have the choice of planting. Cost is a great element in making choices. Seeding a lawn is the cheapest method and sodding a lawn is the most expensive. Turf that runs can be sprigged, placing it in the middle of seeding and sodding in cost.

Gothic grass is my term for a mix of lawn ingredients: clover, fescue, dwarf chamomile, tiny wildflowers, dwarf daffodils, crocus and more. Use Gothic grass with older homes and enjoy the fragrance, beauty and varied good insects.

ABOVE: Two lawn paths intersect adding formal structure to this garden.

OPPOSITE: A circular lawn path leads to a serene resting place.

"When you better your home, you better your life."

– Karol Dewulf Nickell

ABOVE: Meadows create wonderful songbird habitats.
Paths in meadows can be as simple as these wood chips.

Meadows

Small or large meadows make romantic garden paths. Plant mixes for seeding meadows vary by region. Meadows are low maintenance, requiring less mowing and water than lawns, and very good for the environment. Meadows can be formal or informal depending on the artistry of how they are mown. Mow a low, straight strip in your meadow, leading to a circle mowed lower. Place a beautiful pot on a plinth at the exact center of the circle and you have just recreated a meadow seen at a castle in Scotland. Scent meadows attract a diversity of insects making them alluring to the foot and eye. Add grasses to the mix and your meadow will be pleasing to the ear during winter. If you are beginning your meadow with a canned mix be sure you are not seeding invasive plants.

OPPOSITE: A meadow is a blank canvas for a pathway. Mow a low strip wherever you want a path. Paths through meadows cast deep shadows during full moons.

Groundcovers

Areas planted in groundcover are less formal than a lawn more formal than a meadow. Groundcovers are not a good choice for busy paths. You can remedy this by adding a path of stepping stones through the groundcover area. Lightly traveled areas can tolerate a simple groundcover path. The best choices are spreading plants that tolerate poor soil, light foot traffic, and are evergreen. Be sure to choose the proper groundcover for the amount of sunlight it will receive.

If a lawn is your path but stops growing where it is too shady you will have to complete the effect with a groundcover.

ABOVE: Groundcovers hold the soil around a path and make a new path look old quickly, sometimes within one year.

ABOVE: This turf path is aesthetic and functional leading to the front door.

Mulch Paths

Mulch paths vary by region, depending on the material that is available. Mulch paths can be pine straw, shredded leaves, wood chips, shredded tree bark, cocoa shells and etc. Many tree cutting services provide shredded mulch free. Mulch can be spread on bare dirt. These types of paths will degrade over time and need replenishing. Unusual mulch can be aesthetically pleasing but a struggle to find through the years. It's best to use what is consistently available. A three-inch thickness of natural mulch is good for most garden paths. To determine the amount of material to buy, multiply the length of the path times the width in feet. Then multiply the result by the depth in feet to determine the cubic footage required.

Installing a Wood Chip Path

Wood chips are sold by the bag or might be free from a local tree service company.

1. Clear new path area and lay string at its outer edges to visualize. Make your path at least 2½ feet wide.

2. If soldiers are used, install them first. Spread wood chips three inches deep.

3. If spreading wood chips by the bag, place bags end to end along path. Cut bags open along one end and slide wood chips out. Rake smooth.

4. If spreading wood chips from a large mound, shovel into wheelbarrow, roll to path, dump. Rake smooth. Repeat.

"Poetry often enters through the window of irrelevance."

- M.C. Richards

Gravel Paths

Gravel paths are cheap when bought by the ton, not by the bag, and long lasting. To estimate how much gravel you will need, measure your path to get the square footage. Place your gravel order by requesting X amount of gravel to cover your square footage two inches deep. An easy material to use gravel can be spread on bare dirt. Replenish as it settles. Edging a gravel path is important to keep it in place. Bricks, stones and metal all look good edging gravel.

Gravel paths are not a good choice for people with small children. Children have gravel DNA, telling them to "pick up and throw." Small gravel is not a good choice for cold climates where it can stick to the bottom of shoes during icy weather and brought inside to damage flooring.

Maintenance is a necessity for gravel paths. Using pre-emergents and post-emergents to prevent weeds is helpful. Debris in gravel paths can be cleared with a rake and blower.

ABOVE: Crushed gravel, leading in a formal, straight line to the front door. Before you enter this front door its pathway has already created a good first impression.

"Beware, rough gravel,

commom to parking lots,

an make your garden

seem like a parking lot."

ABOVE: Rough stone gravel, the edges are rough not smooth like pea gravel. Rough gravel comes in many sizes. Rough gravel, used wisely, can be attractive in a garden. Beware, rough gravel, common to parking lots, can make your garden seem like a parking lot.

RIGHT: Pea gravel comes in several sizes, its surface is irregular but smoothly rounded.

Stone Gravel

Small stone gravel, any smaller and it would be gravel grit, great for small gardens but bad for getting caught in shoe treads.

The most common stone gravel size for paths.

Stone Gravel

Broken stone, with jagged edges, comes in various sizes from $^1/_4$ inch to 5 inches. The smaller sizes are best for garden paths. Stone gravel larger than $^1/_2$ inch will make a garden path look like a parking lot because sizes above $^1/_2$ inch are commonly used for commercial stone gravel parking lots.

ABOVE: Probably the largest size stone gravel suitable for residential garden paths. Larger stone gravel will create the look of a commercial site.

Pea Gravel - Small, Medium & Large

This pathway material comes in various sizes and colors with a rounded exterior, no sharp edges. Small gardens look best with small ¼ inch pea gravel. Small pea gravel has a very informal aesthetic. Medium sized pea gravel, ¾ inch, is the easiest to find and most commonly used. It leans toward informal but can look formal with raised brick edging. Large, egg-sized pea gravel is difficult to walk on in high heels. It can appear impersonal or commercial in a residential setting. Light-colored pea gravel radiates the liquid mercury light of a full moon, bright enough to read by.

Pea gravel laid directly on dirt will be similar to walking on sand, initially. As the pea gravel settles it becomes firmer to walk upon. For the first six to eight years a pea gravel path will need to be replenished a small amount every other year, as it settles into the soil.

Shoes for working along a pea gravel path are best without cleats, which may pick-up the gravel and carry it inside, damaging floors.

Pea Gravel

Best for small gardens.

Most commonly used in formal and informal gardens.

May appear commercial in a residential path

Gravel Paths

Installing Gravel Paths

1. Determine where your path will be. Laying string along the outer edges of the path will let you see it and use it before construction.

2. If the area becoming pathway is currently lawn remove the lawn with a sod cutter or hand tools. (See photo1.)

3. Measure the length and width of your path. Multiply length by width to get square footage.

4. Order gravel by requesting enough to cover your square footage two inches deep. Sold by the ton, gravel is much cheaper in bulk than by the bag.

5. Plan a location site for gravel delivery closest to its installation site. Use caution – gravel delivery on lawns, due to weight, will kill your lawn. Use tarp under gravel pile.

6. If soldiers are being used install them first.

7. Shovel gravel into wheelbarrow, roll to new path, dump, repeat. Carry empty tarp to new path and shake. (See photo 2.)

ABOVE: Preparing for a new path and dumping pea gravel.

"Every moment of one's existence one is growing into more or retreating into less."

- Norman Mailer

ABOVE: Pea gravel paths can be easily blown for maintenance and also look refreshed after a raking.

Stone

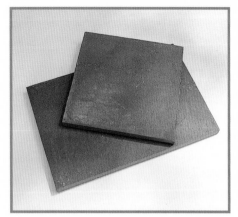

Cut stone has a formal look and is available in numerous types and sizes.

Field stone is commonly used in formal and informal gardens.

Granite block is useful for edging many types of paths.

Stone Paths

Depending on how it is laid, stone pathways can be formal or informal. Using small stones, 10 - 11 inches wide placed 6 - 7 inches apart creates a very informal path. Placing large stones, 16 - 24 inches across, rectangular in shape and closely together creates a formal path. Edging a stone path with brick or cobblestone raised two inches higher than the pathway stones creates a formal path.

Stone is relatively cheap in most regions. Choose stone that is strong and won't crumble over time. Flat stone, 1inch thick and approximately 16 inches wide is best for pathways. Stone can be laid on bare soil. Many reference materials say to place stones 2 - 3 inches apart for pathways, I prefer stepping stones to be 1 inch apart for easy walking and the ability to plant between stones. Place stones so you won't have to look down while walking.

Making young gardens look older is a prized attribute of stone. Cut into geometric shapes and laid in a pattern, stone pathways can become a year-round focal point. Stone, laid in dirt, may have to be adjusted over time to remain flat.

OPPOSITE: Lawns are great pathways but need help in heavily trafficked lanes. Laying stone in lawns is intriguing; at different angles the stones cannot be seen. It is less maintenance to lay stone in clumping grasses than in running grasses. Running grasses quickly grow over stone if not pruned regularly.

Installing a Stepping Stone Path in Stone Grit

Stone is sold by the ton and arrives on pallets when purchased in bulk. Stone can also be purchased by the piece. When purchasing stone by the piece bring work gloves. Many stone centers will not have a salesperson pull individual stones for you.

1. Lay string along the outer edges of the new path, or use spray paint, for visualization. (See photo 1.)

2. Estimate the number of stepping stones needed. Assume they are placed one inch apart. Walk the path counting each closely placed footstep. Add five stones to the step count for every ten steps. Too many stones are better than too few.

3. Choose stones that are $\frac{1}{2}$- 1 inch thick and 18 - 30 inches wide, and level on top and bottom. Stones not level will wobble when walked on.

4. Dig the length of the new path to a depth 50-70% the thickness of your stone. (See photo 2.) If you've decided to use soldiers place them first.

5. Place your stones one to two inches apart with the largest prettiest stone at the beginning and another at its destination.

6. Spread stone grit around stones, tamp, moisten, repeat.

7. Allow your new path to dry completely before use. (See photo 4.)

ABOVE: Using mostly gravel in this flagstone path reduces the expense, it is also functional and pretty.

RIGHT: A flagstone path with gravel in the seams, reversing the path idea pictured above. Using the same ingredients but switching the percentages is inline with keeping a garden simple.

Stone Paths

LEFT & BOTTOM LEFT: Two views of the same stone path. A combination of formal and informal with the curving stone path leading to an iron gate, past stone retaining walls, and through lush lawn. The stone path unites the entire area.

BELOW & OPPOSITE: Two views of the same stone path and steps. Irregular stones, informal, were chosen to contrast with the formal garden. The path is not only beautiful it transports you through the garden to a hot tub at one end and a dining room/conservatory at the other.

Stone Path

TOP LEFT: Paths age faster in shade. This path, copying the style of Williamsburg, Virginia, which copied the style of England, which copied the style of… Mixing brick and stone this shady path aged quickly, less than five years, with different types of moss. This path is more for looking at from upstairs windows than for walking on, making the moss acceptable. Some mosses are slick on bricks and stones and should not be encouraged on heavily used paths.

TOP RIGHT: With plantings lushly softening the edges of these stepping stones it's easy to deduce the gardener must have disliked how formal the path looked when it was new and the plantings were young. If this is the style path you want know that you'll have to be patient, 3-4 years, before you get the look you're after.

BOTTOM LEFT: A very slight slope is part of this path and the steps getting you up the slope are almost imperceptible. It is desirable to have flat areas of path and steps, more drama. Steps are subtle focal points.

OPPOSITE: This stone path has become a small patio too. Wherever you might like to add seating in your garden consider using this technique of creating a small patio that is also a path.

Stone Paths

ABOVE: These steps were made by first cutting into the hill side to make way for the thick stone slabs. Approximately a third of each stone was then buried in the ground and tamped for stability. When you complete any path, flat or on a slope, spread mulch immediately. Rain can unravel hours of work in minutes.

ABOVE: Path and patio, formal with square cut stones, informal with loose pea gravel in the spaces between stones. If grass won't grow near the back or side of your home this would be a pretty solution.

Stone Paths

RIGHT: Here stone soldiers line a wood chip path. Pathways in small areas can make the area appear larger if the path begins wide then tapers several inches, inward, at its end. Use small leaved plantings along the path; large leaves make a garden appear smaller. Wood chips can be purchased by the bag or requested from a tree cutting service. Most will deliver large piles free.

BELOW: Stones set in concrete should be carefully done so cracks don't develop in the concrete. Northern climates need a deeper base of concrete than Southern climates.

TOP LEFT: A path for convenience. The turf is near, and could be the path, but this gardener knows how the garden is used; these stones were laid creating a path to the upper level. Always choose what is practical.

TOP RIGHT: Every path is important no matter how short. Put more effort into a path of 3 feet than 300 feet.

ABOVE: Beginning wide then tapering towards its destination, this path makes a small area appear larger. The path and its plantings also give an incredible first impression of anything to be found just inside the door.

Brick Paths

Brick paths can be elegant and formal or charming and informal. It is best to use bricks that are solid, without holes, so slugs won't have a breeding ground. If bricks, with holes, are left-over from the construction of your house, use them dug into the dirt or with concrete to cover the holes. If your house isn't brick' choose brick that is harmonious with the architecture of the house. A house with brick should have, if possible, the same brick used in its garden. Brick can be laid in soil, level sand, or concrete.

CLOCKWISE FROM TOP LEFT: Bricks in concrete, with soldiers flush, in a broad curve. Bricks in concrete with no soldiers. Bricks set in dirt and turf. A charming footpath for guests walking from car to front door.

OPPOSITE: Bricks welcome you at this front door. Laid in concrete; they could have been laid in soil with creeping thyme growing in the cracks for a different look.

Installing Brick in Soil

1. Determine exact area to be used with string or spray paint.

2. Collect bricks and tools such as a flat edge shovel, a broom, a rake and edging tool. (See photos 1 & 2.)

3. Dig area to proper depth, commonly 50-70% the height of your bricks. Level and compact the soil to ensure the path surface will be reasonably flat. (See photo 3.)

4. Place bricks in the desired pattern taking care to raise or lower any bricks that may lay too high or too low. (See photo 4.)

5. Sweep loose soil across the surface to fill in the cracks and secure the bricks. (See photos 5 & 6.)

6. Tamp soil between the bricks. (See photo 7.)

7. Apply water, allow it to settle. Repeat. (See photo 8.)

"Bricks with holes are sex shacks for slugs."

PHOTOS 1 & 2: Gather supplies and tools.
PHOTO 3: Dig the base.

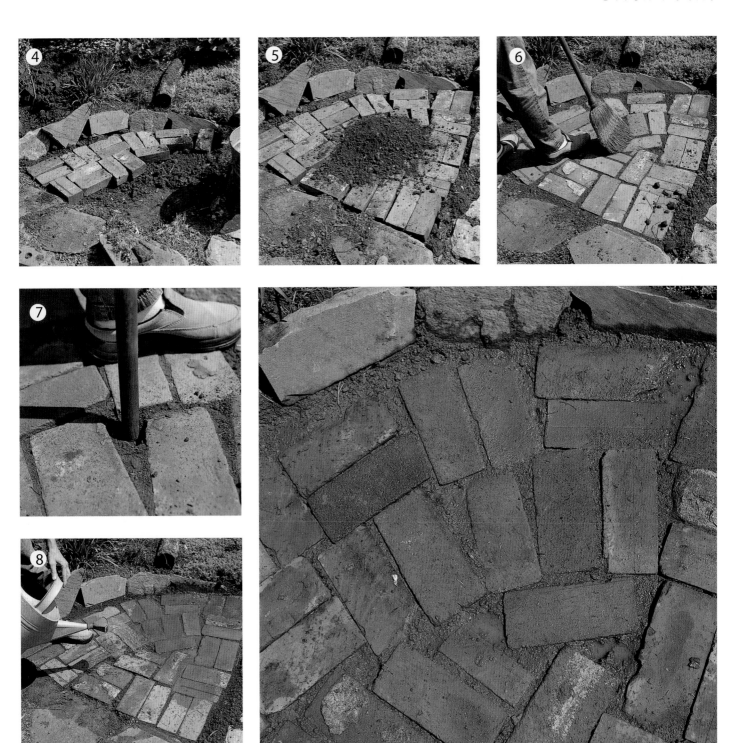

PHOTO 4: Lay the brick, preferrably with no holes showing.
PHOTO 5 & 6: Spread soil and sweep into cracks.
PHOTO 7 & 8: Tamping the soil and watering it down.
ABOVE: The new path, seconds old.

Wood Paths

Wood

Common railroad ties are used as garden steps, retaining walls and path edging.

Pressure treated wood is used for garden steps, retaining walls and path edging. Wood can be stained a variety of colors.

ABOVE: Railroad tie were choosen for these high traffic steps.

Paths made of wood are usually found in sites that are steep or boggy. Boardwalks are not long lasting but are a cheaper solution than stone, brick or concrete. Railroad ties have about a 30-year life; pressure treated wood somewhat less.

Boardwalks, like pressure treated wood used for steps or edging, can be stained to match an element of your house. Railroad ties do not take stain well, but can look beautiful when camouflaged with plantings.

Using tree limbs to edge woodland, or informal paths, is an old concept and looks best when the limbs are a minimum of two inches in diameter and of varying lengths – about four to eight feet long.

ABOVE: Boardwalk paths are a good solution to areas that are steep or boggy.

Wood Paths

ABOVE: A simple wooden bridge allows the path to continue over a small creek. This bridge is formed with three 4″ x 6″ pressure treated beams and decked with pressure treated five quarter planks.

OPPOSITE: Railroad ties are used to form the structure of this path and pavers provide the actual walking surface.

Concrete Paths

Concrete, not boring anymore, can be stained a wide variety of colors and stamped into different patterns. Less than three decades ago many gardeners made their own concrete stepping stones. Time and cost was outweighed by cheaper ready-made concrete stepping stones in choices of size, color and pattern.

ABOVE: A new concrete path, stamped and stained. Details of this path: mixing, pouring, shaping, staining, leveling, stamping and its length make it beyond the realm of most do-it-yourselfers.

OPPOSITE: Concrete paving squares set in pea gravel lead to a rear garden and pool area. The path begins with an engraved granite stone.

This Garden is in loving memory of
my beloved mother

❧

Jane Elizabeth Norris
2003

ABOVE: A pathway of lawn and a pathway of concrete and stone lead to this front door. The concrete and stone path are expected but the turf path is an added surprise, functional and aesthetic.

Atlanta Botanical Garden

Interlocking Pavers

Interlocking pavers, sold for many years, have had an image consultant. New styles and patterns create pathways with the look of more expensive stone or brick. Setting interlocking pavers in sand or grit requires patience, skill and time. It can't be a do-it-yourself job for the back yard but it is a job best contracted with professionals for the look in the photo above.

LEFT: Interlocking pavers informally melding into a lush setting quite naturally. ABOVE: Interlocking pavers formally curving to a front door.

"I'd be hard-pressed to understand one thing that has more effect on our lives than our built environment."

– Bruce Lindsey

ABOVE: Interlocking pavers set in sand create a tight fit, choking out most weeds and allowing water to drain through.

Garden Paths of China and Japan

"If something is good once it's always good."

– Van Day Truex

Japanese Gardens

Spirituality is intensified in a Japanese garden. Every plant, rock and grain of sand is imbued with spiritual meaning. Spiritual ties dictate much of Japanese garden design. Formal pathways will be of cut stones; less formal pathways will be a mix of cut stones and natural stones. The simplest of paths in a courtyard will be of sand. Pathways leading to a tea house in a Japanese garden are meant to be contemplative, helping those on the path to leave worldly thoughts behind so spiritual enlightenment can be experienced. Japanese gardening evolved by absorbing Chinese ideas close to 300 AD.

PICTURED RIGHT: Garden entrance with a path luring both the eye and foot. Notice the contrasts in this small space: rigid, straight fence outlining jagged irregularly placed stepping stones and loose gravel, differing colors of foliage and leaf types. No element was chosen without great consideration.

Atlanta Botanical Garden

"Herbs and trees, stones and rocks shall all enter into Nirvana."

- Buddhist Proverb

Atlanta Botanical Garden

Chinese Gardens

Naturalistic gardens are the Chinese style, dating past the Han Dynasty, 206BC-220AD. They amplify nature by creating mountains, lakes, streams, meadows and winding paths that fashion beautiful compositions with spiritual reverence. Unfortunately, most early naturalistic Chinese gardens went back to nature when their owner died; it was common practice for a family to move when the patriarch died. English gardener Christopher Lloyd has said, "The garden dies when the gardener dies."

ABOVE: Is the curving path through this Asian style garden flowing like a stream or a cow path? Both. Path and garden are cohesive, creating a garden with strong but few elements, loaded with metaphors of nature and spirituality.

OPPOSITE: This pathway is more beautiful because it had a challenge – water. Designed to mimic a water bridge, this stepping stone path beautifully solves a problem. Enjoy the challenges crossing your paths.

87

ABOVE: An ancient style path, flagstone with gravel, chosen to echo the color of a Japanese Maple. In winter the stems of the Japanese Maple color echo with the path.

RIGHT: Carefully but casually dug-in, these stepping stones that are several inches thick, create a staircase path. No concrete is needed because of the thickness of the stones. Soon, the moss will make the stone steps look like nature placed them instead of man.

ABOVE: This garden path has Oriental origins with its use of gravel, stone and style of placement. Yet other ideas spanning different eras and continents have an influence too. Keep things simple when mixing eras and cultures. Take the very best of what you like then mix.

Chinese & Japanese Gardens

1. Chinese gardens, for over 2000 years have copied nature. Garden paths are winding. Spirituality is important.

2. Japanese gardens copy nature and imbue every element with spirituality.

Western Garden Paths

Knowledge about Chinese and Japanese gardens did not become widely available until the early 18th century in the West. England and the Continent were traveling freely with their ships and sending missionaries, many Jesuit priests, around the globe. Descriptions of Chinese and Japanese gardens were well received, especially in France. Timing was good, Jesuit priests were gaining a toehold in the Chinese culture and French design masters Le Brun and Le Notre were dead by 1700. Suddenly the glories of the gardens at Versailles, with its straight garden paths, became outdated. With Chinese and Japanese influence the French enjoyed 50 years of rococo gardens, the wild, flowing lines adapted from Chinese and Japanese meandering paths. Rococo faded after discovery of the gardens at Pompeii with classic, straight lines harking back to the Persian influence.

ABOVE: Stones cut formally and laid formally with lush plantings spilling over the edges adding informality.

OPPOSITE: It's no surprise this garden is exciting, so much has been mixed. The path, curving through a formal lawn, takes you to a formal clipped topiary garden, past less formal shrubs at the edge of the woodland and finally into the forest primeval. Any garden is at its most exciting when formal and informal are in close proximity. Add a path uniting the two and you'll get magic.

"Five woodland walks pass upward through the trees; every one has its own character, while the details change during its progress-never abruptly, but in leisurely sequence; as if inviting the quiet stroller to stop a moment to enjoy some little woodland suavity, and then gently enticing him to go further, with agreeable anticipation of what might come next."

– Gertrude Jekyll, 1921

Chinese and Japanese garden ideas also spread quickly in England. With naturalists Lancelot "Capability" Brown (1715-1783) and Humphrey Repton (1752-1818) the first to advertise his services as "landscape gardener", centuries of formal gardens having straight paths were confidently destroyed to create gardens copying nature with ideas from the East.

English garden designer Gertrude Jekyll (1843-1932) created a new garden style; gardens with different "rooms," formal areas with straight paths and natural areas with winding paths. Because she was English her ideas had the reach of an Empire. After Jekyll, Hollywood has been a huge purveyor of garden ideas followed by TV, magazines, books and the Internet.

ABOVE: Neo-formality in a woodland garden. Most trees limbed-up with higher branches remaining. Meandering paths arepaved with rough stone gravel. It has a huge impact with little yearly labor to maintain or expense to create.

OPPOSITE: This path winds through low plantings. The steps are anchored by ground cover. The path leads to another garden room.

"The lights are going out all over Europe.
We shall not see them lit again in our lifetime."

– Sir Edward Grey at the start of WWI

A common garden path today, flagstones caressed by foliage, is not yet a century old. Prior to WWI labor was cheap. Established gardens across Europe had flagstone terraces that were maintained cheaply. Economics of wartime and a shortage of laborers changed those flagstone terraces and the style of garden they were in. Unable to properly weed and repoint the mortar between stones, bare flagstone terraces became new garden space. Desirable plants that sprouted were kept in an effort to choke out undesirable weeds. Suddenly, terraces were beautiful again. It was a different kind of beauty, attracting many gardeners to copy what they saw.

ABOVE: It's automatic in our era to create stone paths with plantings growing between the cracks, a style not yet a century old. Choose the correct plantings for your path. They must be low growing, able to handle foot traffic and spreading to choke out weeds.

ABOVE: Too soften the formal lines of this straight stone path, and rectangular terrace, two inch stones were laid in dirt, one inch apart, for plants to grow. Charm arrives with what the wind plants. If you don't like uninvited guests growing in your cracks, pull them before they bloom or you will have their children too.

Front Yard Pathways

"Expressing personal feelings and memories is the essence of decorating."

– Sister Parrish

A pathway to your front door should accommodate two people walking abreast, five feet is generously ample. Martha Schwartz, adjunct professor at Harvard Design School says, "The problem is that our notion of the quality of life ends at our front door." She's right, design the same quality of life you have inside your home out to the property line. Create a moat of grace. Don't just have the bare necessities for a path in your front yard. Have paths that allow you to circulate your entire property. William Shakespeare agrees too, "Self-love…is not so vile a sin as self-neglecting." Not having paths in your garden, taking you where you need to go is self-neglect.

Pathways in your front yard for maintenance can be as simple as 1¹/₂ foot stepping stones. Other paths, providing transportation to the sides of your home should be wider, three feet or more.

ABOVE AND RIGHT: This gracious front yard path is in harmony with both the house and garden, aesthetic and functional. A sharp edge along the turf, following the path, creates a frame for the path. Because this pathway is stone it could be as old as the house or completed last month.

Your house and garden should be harmonious in materials. Get the selection correct because a first impression takes three seconds. If your home is brick, use the same brick to make your pathways. Brick pathways can be expensive; to economize, use bricks as edging with cheaper gravel or stone. Crushed brick is similar in texture and sound to gravel paths but more elegant in effect.

Gray flagstone is a classic choice for garden paths, durable and aesthetic, it looks fabulous with a cedar prairie style home or formal red brick Georgian manor.

ABOVE: The curving lines of this path contrast nicely with the many straight architectural lines of the house. The house is expanded beyond its walls with the path.

OPPOSITE: Part of a complete art piece, this path leads foot and eye to the focal point of the front yard, the front door. With no element unconsidered, this front yard makes me want to investigate the entire garden and hope that the house is someday open for a tour. Path, house, and garden have created a trinity.

Let function dictate where pathways should go in your front yard then look at those pathways from multiple directions. Don't look at your front yard from just the street view in, look at it from your front windows out, and while driving onto your property in the car. Viewing from multiple directions allows you to add pleasing form to your paths yet keep their primary function intact. Marry form and function with paths, keeping them simple to elevate their structure to art. The mundane is easy to achieve, and with slightly more effort you can achieve beauty.

OPPOSITE: At first glance this front yard and path appear quite proper; the façade drops when you see flagstones placed through the turf, heading to the smaller door at right. The little path exposes some of the personality of those living in the house.

ABOVE: Random slate pieces placed carefully below the turf's surface make an informal path in a formal setting.

101

Front Yard Pathways

LEFT & BELOW: This little path connects a side of the house with the front of the house. Not a major path, it is needed to help the owner maintain the garden with ease. The stones are set in dirt.

LEFT: Simplicity of line, materials and plantings. This path is beautiful in every season and low maintenance.

BELOW: This pathway makes the home look like a vacation retreat with a staff. It also breaks the rule of keeping a diversity of path materials to a minimum. Most paths are best when made of one or two types of material. This path proves that breaking rules with gusto does have rewards. For most front yards, having a pea gravel path lead to a wooden bridge, to neatly cut slate, to irregularly cut stone would be chaos, here it's beautiful.

"Well begun is half done."

— Aristotle

Front Yard Pathways

1. Front door pathways should accommodate two people walking abreast; five feet is ample.

2. Front yard paths, not leading to a door, can be three feet wide.

3. A small maintenance path, infrequently used, can be a one foot stepping-stone.

4. House and garden should have harmonious materials.

5. Gray flagstone is a classic pathway choice for formal and informal homes.

6. Keep the diversity of materials minimal.

7. Repetition of path materials is important.

8. Push the limits of any garden design rule.

9. Create repetition within a diversity of materials.

10. Function should dictate where pathways go.

11. View your pathways from multiple perspectives to help you add pleasing form.

12. Marry form and function with your paths to elevate their structure to art.

ABOVE: Brick edging along paths, matching the bricks on the house, unite house and garden.

Back Yard Pathways

In your back yard you will need pathways three to five feet wide, leading to doors that are used as access to family living and entertaining. Other back yard pathways should be three feet wide, with narrower paths $1^1/_2$ - 2 feet for infrequent maintenance use. Make sure paths carrying wheelbarrows and lawn mowers are wide enough. Don't make paths wider than needed. Gardens with acreage can have paths too wide creating a garden that looks commercial. Paths with broad curves enlarge a garden and are graceful. Creating pathways that are extremely wavy, with short curves splinter a garden, becoming ugly focal points.

Front yards automatically have a focal point, your house and front door. A back yard is mostly viewed from the house out, making pathways a beautiful focal point. If there is any place you need to go in your back yard, create a path but don't create more paths than necessary. Pathways are an invitation, combining form and function.

OPPOSITE & ABOVE: Taming woodland back yards with pathways of stone and gravel. Gravel is inexpensive and handles cheaply too; it doesn't require skilled labor. Gravel has proven useful in gardens for hundreds of years.

ABOVE: Pathways in this back yard let you know the back yard is for living. It also extends the architecture of the house. Plantings, around the large stones set in soil, stabilize soil and help the stone remain in place for decades. There is no rule against having beautiful plants perform tough jobs.

OPPOSITE: Paths in this back yard allow you to circulate the perimeter, crisscross its interior, and leave by either side of the house. The paths allow you to also enter any of the back doors.

Back Yard Pathways

The further a path travels from the house the less formal it can become. What begins as a solid brick path can change to wood chips edged with bricks then finally just wood chips. Keeping pathways harmonious while transitioning ingredients makes even small back yards feel larger. Walking from a pond to the compost pile, to a tiny lawn, to the woodland path, to the gazebo, with varying harmonious path ingredients makes you feel as if you have traveled to many interesting areas, because you have. Each area has its own room with its own character.

If your garden space is small, create pathways that look longer than they are. Do this by beginning the pathway wider at its front and tapering narrower at its end.

While on a pathway far in your back yard, look back at your house. Consider this view your lake view and you're in a boat. Suddenly the back of your house becomes another front. Many new ideas should come to you while thinking from this perspective. Does the back of your house need shutters, new light fixtures, lush plantings, and better paths?

ABOVE: These steps, stones set in concrete, make the pea gravel paths appear more formal than they are. Stone mixes well with most other ingredients for making paths.

ABOVE: These formal stone steps lead to a less formal stone path through the woods. Having the path set in dirt and planted with groundcovers between the cracks emphasizes the boundary of formal and informal. This is a desirable garden design technique.

RIGHT: A new stone path. Most garden pictures have pathways with mature plantings; you can copy a path exactly yet it won't look the way you want until year three or beyond.

Back Yard Pathways

TOP: The slope in this back yard would be too steep without adding stepping stones to the path.

RIGHT: These back yard pathways were built wide enough for a tractor to drive along. Always consider the width of anything traveling along your paths: boat, trailer, lawn mower, tractor, wheelbarrow and etc.

OPPOSITE: This back yard pathway leads to a bench within a sanctuary. Create destinations along longer pathways.

LEFT: A path leading from back yard to side yard. Foot traffic needs to flow freely around your entire property. This path was a dead-end until the fence had an opening cut. What was a dead-end is now an entryway.

Plants radiate serenity and grace, as we order our gardens the serenity and grace are amplified.

Back Yard Pathway Considerations:

🌿 Paths leading to doors for family living and entertaining should be three to five feet wide.

🌿 Pathways not leading to doors should be $2^1/_2$ - 3 feet wide.

🌿 Maintenance paths can range from one to three feet wide.

🌿 Don't make paths wider than needed.

🌿 Paths with broad curves enlarge a garden and are graceful.

🌿 Extremely wavy paths splinter a garden and become ugly focal points.

ABOVE: Before the fence was cut this area had two dead-ends now the same area has two entryways. An accidental benefit of creating this new path is how beautiful it looks from upstairs windows.

Back Yard Pathway Considerations:

🌿 Back yard pathways create a focal point.

🌿 Create paths to anyplace you need to go in your back yard.

🌿 Pathways are an invitation.

🌿 Remember to combine form and function.

🌿 The further a path travels from the house the less formal it can become.

🌿 Keeping pathways harmonious, while transitioning ingredients makes small back yards feel larger.

🌿 Making a pathway larger at its beginning and smaller at its end makes a small garden appear larger.

🌿 The view to your house, from the back property line, should be as pretty as its opposite view.

OPPOSITE & ABOVE: A view from side yard to back yard. Billowing flowering shrubs create different views along the path.

ABOVE: A tiny side yard woodland path inviting you to travel from front to back with rapt interest. The area is tiny so this path is only two feet wide, made of wood chips edged with fallen tree limbs. This tiny garden has a big job, hiding the air-conditioner and providing beautiful views from inside the house. There are so many plants along this path that the birds fly through using the line of the path.

OPPOSITE: Under the deep eaves of this house a path is a better choice than plantings, which would not get rain water.

Formal Garden Paths

"Ancient Greeks called proportion the soul of what we see."

– Alexandra Stoddard

A straight or broadly curving path, five feet wide, made of stone, brick or concrete with an edging is considered formal. Don't be afraid of formal. Formal garden paths are low maintenance. If you don't like the severe lines a formal path creates, let lush plantings flow lightly or exuberantly over the edges of the path.

What is meant by formal is a relative term. Flagstone, a formal paving material, becomes informal when it is laid in sand or mulch rather than with concretemortared joints. Your favorite path might be two to three feet wide, of plain dirt, edged with groundcovers on each side. A wood chip path five feet wide, edged with four inch diameter tree limbs would be formal to you. Someone else liking a straight path, four feet wide, of stone edged with brick would be mystified at the thought of any wood chip path being formal. Play with the idea of formal and informal paths in your garden. It's preferable to have both.

ABOVE: A tiny courtyard garden with a substantial, and wide pathway indicating heavy use.

ABOVE: Stone steps invite you to another part of the garden. Generously wide and dressed with potted plants, the path speaks to feet and eyes. How beautiful this path must be when it is raining.

Formal Garden Paths

RIGHT: Small vegetable and herb gardens have been designed this way for centuries. Straight paths around each bed allow for easy maintenance. Loosely setting the stones also allows next season's crops to be laid out in a different configuration for crop rotation.

BELOW: A formal herb garden with brick pathway and matching wall. Notice how most of the bed space is easily worked while keeping feet on the pathway. Continually placing feet in your beds for maintenance will compact soil.

Atlanta Botanical Garden

LEFT: A good example of a main pathway, branching off, with a side path. It's interesting how others decide to move foot traffic.

BELOW: A pathway enfilade, a view through to a view. This path directs the eye to the urn, then beyond to a bench. Whenever you can use a path to lead the eye toward two or more focal points you have created an enfilade. This is very sophisticated.

Atlanta Botanical Garden

ABOVE: Dirt path winding through a fern glade to a footbridge, and beyond, into the woodland. If many people won't be walking through your fern glade, a dirt and humus path is the preferred choice. Remember what the Chinese have done for thousands of years – copy nature.

LEFT: This path, not new and not yet mature, is a good example of how to plant along your paths. Groundcovers should be one inch or less at stones. Graduate the plant sizes, small to large, as you move farther away from the path into the bed.

LEFT: The groundcover planted at this stone path's edge is important. It will spread and hold the soil for stone laid in dirt. When planning the materials for your paths also plan which groundcovers will be planted. If you can't plant groundcovers, when your path is installed, be sure to spread a three inch layer of mulch to hold the soil.

BELOW: Notice where the corners meet in this square slate path. Laying the corners in a "T" creates a stronger path.

Formal Garden Paths

ABOVE: This formal rectangular cut stone has unusual soldiers, six by six inch wood posts. A mix of formal and informal leading you through the woods.

LEFT: An old idea, the roundabout, created with stamped, stained concrete.

ABOVE: Many styles of cut stone meet at this stairway, formality leading to informality. Planting a low groundcover on the stone steps intensifies the informality. When formal areas meet informal areas, show off the differences.

Informal Garden Paths

"Creative life always stands outside convention."

– Carl Jung

Informal paths refer to walkways that are irregular and winding rather than straight. They have Informal garden paths can be a few flagstones leading to a water faucet through a shrub border; a dirt path in a woodland leading to the compost pile; or pea gravel edged with brick leading to a flagstone terrace. Informal is a relative term, just as formal is, when designing your garden pathways. Any path can be made informal by the plantings placed at its edges and how far they are allowed to grow onto the path. Informal garden paths make a garden feel intimate.

Maintenance is usually greater with informal paths. Wood chips and pea gravel, if used, need to be replenished and also contained within their edges. Cost is less for informal garden paths because skilled labor isn't required to clear a dirt path, shovel wood chips or pour wheelbarrows of pea gravel. Informal paths, especially if you make them yourself, add an element of charm to gardens. They also have an element of folk art.

ABOVE: This formal style house needed a path to get from the front yard to the back. After noticing that a path was being worn in the grass, the owner placed this casual stone path.

OPPOSITE: Is this path formal or informal? The answer is relative; when compared to a dirt path through humus this path is formal, when compared to the same path with cobblestones lining the edge it is informal. Initially more expensive than lawn this path and plantings, if the owner remains 10 years, will be much cheaper than lawn.

Informal Garden Paths

ABOVE & LEFT: When planting groundcovers around your stepping stones, be sure to choose plants that can tolerate being stepped on. When groundcovers become mature, maintenance might include one to three times of weed-eating each year.

ABOVE: This wild wood has been designed to be an outdoor art museum. Keeping the path of dirt and planting native plants creates a potent backdrop for any art piece you display.

OPPOSITE: This path has a drop off on its left side so handrails were installed. Keeping with the woodland aesthetics, impervious locust wood was chosen to make the rail.

TOP: Using what the land provided, this woodland path has been cleared of its stones, which have been used as soldiers.

LEFT: Moss growing around path stones is a yearly treat as it turns different colors from summer to winter.

ABOVE: This pathway has had help with plantings from the wind, the fern is a volunteer. Providence, many times, is a better planter than we are.

OPPOSITE: Having a beautiful front yard and back yard meant that this gardener needed to create a beautiful side yard path for access to both.

Informal Garden Paths

RIGHT: This pathway has a miniature garden around each stone. When creating a miniature garden for each of your stepping stones, be sure to contrast foliage colors and textures.

BELOW: This classic stone path was made unique when man-made resin stepping stones were added to the mix.

ABOVE & LEFT: A copy of nature on a dry, sunny slope. This entire garden becomes a path.

ABOVE: For children only. These stone steps were cut into a steep slope leading to a small pruned opening in the evergreen hedge, creating a shortcut to another part of the garden. Too steep and small for adults, the children adore having their private path.

RIGHT: If you have a woodland path, use what the woodland provides. Here the gardener put a curving tree limb into the curve of a path.

OPPOSITE PAGE: Its square cut slate would normally be considered formal. Set diagonally in gravel lessens the formal look, but not the impact of this stunning path.

ABOVE: In this tiny garden area the stone path, through turf, adds impact and encourages a quick perusal of the garden room.

RIGHT: A country herb garden path leading to open meadow. The meadow and its rolling curves create a focal point at the end of the herb garden path.

"In the arts, people are constantly looting the rubbish heaps of history.

The more educated you are, the more you get."

– Jonathan Miller

Creating your own garden stepping stones and paths using the techniques listed in this book places you in kinship with 10,000 years worth of gardeners, allowing you to have a unique garden. An irony of design rules, at first glance we think rules take our individuality away until we pay attention and realize how liberating design rules are.

The garden owner's hands created most of the paths in this book. With advance preparation, many of the paths shown can be created in a weekend. Advance preparation includes having all the supplies on site by Friday afternoon so no time is lost in travel or waiting in line.

Most gardening requires patience to see results, installing pathways is an exception. The day a pathway is completed is the day it is mature, no waiting 3-10 years for it to grow. The paths in this book are aesthetically pleasing, functional and feasible for most budgets.

Be sure to take "before" photographs where your new pathways will be built. The pleasure a garden scrapbook provides only grows.

ABOVE: A new flagstone path at this old house where children and dogs had worn a dirt path.

INDEX

Inches to Millimeters and Centimeters

Inches	MM	CM
1/8	3	.3
1/4	6	.6
3/8	10	1.0
1/2	13	1.3
5/8	16	1.6
3/4	19	1.9
7/8	22	2.2
1	25	2.5
1-1/4	32	3.2
1-1/2	38	3.8
1-3/4	44	4.4
2	51	5.1
3	76	7.6
4	102	10.2
5	127	12.7
6	152	15.2
7	178	17.8
8	203	20.3
9	229	22.9
10	254	25.4
11	279	27.9
12	305	30.5

Yards to Meters

Yards	Meters
1/8	.11
1/4	.23
3/8	.34
1/2	.46
5/8	.57
3/4	.69
7/8	.80
1	.91
2	1.83
3	2.74
4	3.66
5	4.57
6	5.49
7	6.40
8	7.32
9	8.23
10	9.14

A FEW TERMS

BAGH - Persian word meaning house-and-garden

BED - typically covered with mulch or groundcovers and having shrubs and/or perennials, trees

DIVERSITY - a mix of path materials, brick/stone/gravel/wood chips and etc…

EYE-SWEET LINE - broad curving paths that animals create and gardeners copy

FLOW - paths should traverse entirely around your home

FOLLY - a path destination, commonly a temple/tea house/hermitage/ summer house, whimsical

FUN - gardening

GROUNDCOVERS - less formal than a lawn more formal than a meadow

MULCH - commonly organic, spread to hold soil and prevent weeds and water loss

PATHS - a track frequently used by man or beast

REPETITION - important to repeat a garden theme

SOLDIERS - edging along paths, brick/stone/tree limbs